LIFE'S LITTLE BOOK OF WISDOM FOR
Grandmothers

Published by Barbour Publishing, Inc., P.O. Box 719, Uhrichsville, Ohio 44683, www.barbourbooks.com

Our mission is to publish and distribute inspirational products offering exceptional value and biblical encouragement to the masses.

Printed in China.

LIFE'S LITTLE BOOK OF WISDOM FOR
Grandmothers

BARBOUR
PUBLISHING

*Grandmas hold our tiny hands
for just a little while. . .
but our hearts forever.*

UNKNOWN

It's faith in something and
enthusiasm for something
that makes a life worth living.

Oliver Wendell Holmes

I AM ALWAYS CONTENT WITH WHAT HAPPENS,
FOR I KNOW THAT WHAT GOD CHOOSES
IS BETTER THAN WHAT I CHOOSE.

EPICTETUS

$\mathcal{T}$HE UNSELFISH EFFORT TO BRING CHEER
TO OTHERS WILL BE THE BEGINNING OF
A HAPPIER LIFE FOR OURSELVES.

HELEN KELLER

I HAVE RESOLVED THAT FROM THIS DAY ON,
I WILL DO ALL THE BUSINESS I CAN HONESTLY,
HAVE ALL THE FUN I CAN REASONABLY,
DO ALL THE GOOD I CAN WILLINGLY, AND SAVE
MY DIGESTION BY THINKING PLEASANTLY.

ROBERT LOUIS STEVENSON

*N*O MATTER WHAT LOOMS AHEAD,
IF YOU CAN EAT TODAY, ENJOY TODAY,
MIX GOOD CHEER WITH FRIENDS TODAY,
ENJOY IT AND BLESS GOD FOR IT.

HENRY WARD BEECHER

Teach us to number our days,
that we may apply our
hearts unto wisdom.

PSALM 90:12

$\mathcal{I}$ HAVE LEARNED THAT SUCCESS
IS MEASURED NOT SO MUCH BY THE
POSITION ONE HAS REACHED IN LIFE
AS BY THE OBSTACLES HE HAS OVERCOME.

BOOKER T. WASHINGTON

$\mathcal{T}$HE IDEAS THAT HAVE LIGHTED MY WAY AND,
TIME AFTER TIME, HAVE GIVEN ME NEW
COURAGE TO FACE LIFE CHEERFULLY HAVE BEEN
KINDNESS, BEAUTY, AND TRUTH.

ALBERT EINSTEIN

No legacy is so rich as honesty.

SHAKESPEARE

*H*AVE COURAGE FOR THE GREAT SORROWS
OF LIFE AND PATIENCE FOR THE SMALL ONES;
AND WHEN YOU HAVE LABORIOUSLY
ACCOMPLISHED YOUR DAILY TASK,
GO TO SLEEP IN PEACE. GOD IS AWAKE.

VICTOR HUGO

A prayer, in its simplest definition,
is merely a wish turned heavenward.

PHILLIPS BROOKS

$\mathcal{D}$O ALL THE GOOD YOU CAN,
BY ALL THE MEANS YOU CAN, IN ALL THE WAYS
YOU CAN, IN ALL THE PLACES YOU CAN, AT ALL THE
TIMES YOU CAN, TO ALL THE PEOPLE YOU CAN,
AS LONG AS EVER YOU CAN.

JOHN WESLEY

*W*E MAKE A LIVING BY WHAT WE GET,
BUT WE MAKE A LIFE BY WHAT WE GIVE.

WINSTON CHURCHILL

Love is the beauty of the soul.

AUGUSTINE

$\mathcal{W}$ITH THE ANCIENT IS WISDOM;
AND IN LENGTH OF DAYS UNDERSTANDING.

JOB 12:12

Knowledge comes, but wisdom lingers.

ALFRED, LORD TENNYSON

$\mathcal{L}$IFE IS A MIRROR;
IF YOU FROWN AT IT, IT FROWNS BACK;
IF YOU SMILE, IT RETURNS THE GREETING.

WILLIAM MAKEPEACE THACKERAY

*D*O NOT PRAY FOR EASY LIVES.
PRAY TO BE STRONGER.
DO NOT PRAY FOR TASKS EQUAL TO YOUR POWERS.
PRAY FOR POWERS EQUAL TO YOUR TASKS.

PHILLIPS BROOKS

*W*HAT LIES BEHIND US AND WHAT
LIES BEFORE US ARE TINY MATTERS
COMPARED TO WHAT LIES WITHIN US.

OLIVER WENDELL HOLMES

I EXPECT TO PASS THROUGH LIFE BUT ONCE.
IF, THEREFORE, THERE CAN BE ANY KINDNESS
I CAN SHOW, OR ANY GOOD THINGS I CAN
DO TO ANY FELLOW HUMAN BEING, LET ME DO
IT NOW AND NOT DEFER IT OR NEGLECT IT,
AS I SHALL NOT PASS THIS WAY AGAIN.

WILLIAM PENN

Once you have learned to love,
you will have learned to live.

Unknown

*M*OST FOLKS ARE ABOUT AS HAPPY AS
THEY MAKE UP THEIR MINDS TO BE.

ABRAHAM LINCOLN

*D*ON'T JUDGE EACH DAY BY THE HARVEST
YOU REAP, BUT BY THE SEEDS YOU PLANT.

ROBERT LOUIS STEVENSON

Be a life long or short, its completeness depends on what it was lived for.

UNKNOWN

*B*EING CONFIDENT OF THIS VERY THING,
THAT HE WHICH HATH BEGUN A GOOD WORK
IN YOU WILL PERFORM IT UNTIL THE DAY
OF JESUS CHRIST.

PHILIPPIANS 1:6

*Children, no matter what their age,
are always hungry when they
go to Grandma's house.*

UNKNOWN

Blessed is the influence of one true, loving human soul on another.

GEORGE ELIOT

I TRY TO AVOID LOOKING FORWARD
OR BACKWARD, AND TRY TO
KEEP LOOKING UPWARD.

CHARLOTTE BRONTË

*H*OW FAR YOU GO IN LIFE DEPENDS ON
YOUR BEING TENDER WITH THE YOUNG,
COMPASSIONATE WITH THE AGED, SYMPATHETIC
WITH THE STRIVING, AND TOLERANT OF THE WEAK
AND THE STRONG. BECAUSE SOMEDAY IN LIFE
YOU WILL HAVE BEEN ALL OF THESE.

GEORGE WASHINGTON CARVER

$\mathcal{W}$HETHER SIXTY OR SIXTEEN, THERE IS IN EVERY
HUMAN BEING'S HEART THE LURE OF WONDER,
THE UNFAILING CHILDLIKE APPETITE OF WHAT'S NEXT,
AND THE JOY OF THE GAME OF LIVING.

SAMUEL ULLMAN

$\mathcal{L}$ET ME BE A WOMAN, HOLY THROUGH AND
THROUGH, ASKING FOR NOTHING BUT WHAT
GOD WANTS TO GIVE ME, RECEIVING WITH
BOTH HANDS AND WITH ALL MY HEART
WHATEVER THAT IS.

ELISABETH ELLIOT

$\mathcal{T}$RUE HAPPINESS COMES WHEN WE STOP
COMPLAINING ABOUT ALL THE TROUBLES
WE HAVE AND OFFER THANKS FOR ALL
THE TROUBLES WE DON'T HAVE.

UNKNOWN

Anyone who has the ability to see beauty never grows old.

FRANZ KAFKA

*W*HO CAN FIND A VIRTUOUS WOMAN?
FOR HER PRICE IS FAR ABOVE RUBIES.

PROVERBS 31:10

*P*EOPLE LIKE YOU AND I, THOUGH MORTAL
OF COURSE LIKE EVERYONE ELSE, DO NOT GROW
OLD NO MATTER HOW LONG WE LIVE. . . .
{WE} NEVER CEASE TO STAND LIKE CURIOUS
CHILDREN BEFORE THE GREAT MYSTERY
INTO WHICH WE WERE BORN.

ALBERT EINSTEIN

Life is God's novel.
Let Him write it.

ISAAC SINGER

I HAVE HELD MANY THINGS IN MY HANDS,
AND I HAVE LOST THEM ALL; BUT WHATEVER
I HAVE PLACED IN GOD'S HANDS,
THAT I STILL POSSESS.

MARTIN LUTHER

True wisdom lies in gathering the precious things out of each day as it goes by.

E. S. BOUTON

*F*AITH IS LIKE A BOOMERANG;
BEGIN USING WHAT YOU HAVE AND IT
COMES BACK TO YOU IN GREATER MEASURE.

CHARLES ALLEN

*T*HE ART OF BEING HAPPY
LIES IN THE POWER OF EXTRACTING
HAPPINESS FROM COMMON THINGS.

HENRY WARD BEECHER

Daily prayers lessen daily cares.

UNKNOWN

GREAT BEAUTY, GREAT STRENGTH,
AND GREAT RICHES ARE REALLY AND TRULY
OF NO GREAT USE; A RIGHT HEART EXCEEDS ALL.

BENJAMIN FRANKLIN

*R*EFLECT UPON YOUR PRESENT BLESSINGS,
OF WHICH EVERY MAN HAS MANY,
NOT ON YOUR PAST MISFORTUNES,
OF WHICH ALL MEN HAVE SOME.

CHARLES DICKENS

I THINK I BEGAN LEARNING LONG AGO
THAT THOSE WHO ARE HAPPIEST ARE THOSE
WHO DO THE MOST FOR OTHERS.

BOOKER T. WASHINGTON

O GIVE THANKS UNTO THE LORD;
FOR HE IS GOOD: FOR HIS MERCY
ENDURETH FOR EVER.

PSALM 136:1

$\mathcal{T}$HE SHORTEST AND SUREST WAY
TO LIVE WITH HONOR IN THE WORLD
IS TO BE IN REALITY WHAT
WE WOULD APPEAR TO BE.

SOCRATES

*One filled with joy
preaches without preaching.*

MOTHER TERESA

*W*E SHOULD ALL DO WHAT,
IN THE LONG RUN, GIVES US JOY,
EVEN IF IT IS ONLY PICKING GRAPES
OR SORTING THE LAUNDRY.

E. B. WHITE

*F*AITH MAKES ALL THINGS POSSIBLE. . . .
LOVE MAKES ALL THINGS EASY.

DWIGHT L. MOODY

What we see depends mainly
on what we look for.

JOHN LUBBOCK

*M*ORE THINGS ARE WROUGHT BY PRAYER
THAN THIS WORLD DREAMS OF.

ALFRED, LORD TENNYSON

The first duty of love is to listen.

PAUL TILLICH

I DON'T BELIEVE MAKEUP AND THE RIGHT HAIRSTYLE ALONE CAN MAKE A WOMAN BEAUTIFUL. THE MOST RADIANT WOMAN IN THE ROOM IS THE ONE FULL OF LIFE AND EXPERIENCE.

UNKNOWN

*M*Y SOUL DOTH MAGNIFY THE LORD,
AND MY SPIRIT HATH REJOICED IN
GOD MY SAVIOUR.

LUKE 1:46-47

*W*E ARE NOT THE SAME PERSONS THIS
YEAR AS LAST; NOR ARE THOSE WE LOVE.
IT IS A HAPPY CHANCE IF WE, CHANGING,
CONTINUE TO LOVE A CHANGED PERSON.

W. SOMERSET MAUGHAM

We are what we repeatedly do.
Excellence, then, is not
an act, but a habit.

ARISTOTLE

My worth to God in public is what I am in private.

OSWALD CHAMBERS

*I*F YOU HAVE KNOWLEDGE,
LET OTHERS LIGHT THEIR CANDLES AT IT.

MARGARET FULLER

*There's no place like home
except Grandma's.*

UNKNOWN

*H*AVE YOU HAD A KINDNESS SHOWN?
PASS IT ON; 'TWAS NOT GIVEN FOR THEE ALONE,
PASS IT ON; LET IT TRAVEL DOWN THE YEARS,
LET IT WIPE ANOTHER'S TEARS,
TILL IN HEAVEN THE DEED APPEARS, PASS IT ON.

HENRY BURTON

*W*HAT DOES IT LOOK LIKE? IT HAS HANDS
TO HELP OTHERS, FEET TO HASTEN TO THE POOR
AND NEEDY, EYES TO SEE MISERY AND WANT,
EARS TO HEAR THE SIGHS AND SORROWS OF MEN.
THAT IS WHAT LOVE LOOKS LIKE.

AUGUSTINE

The reward of a thing well done
is to have done it.

RALPH WALDO EMERSON

*B*Y READING THE SCRIPTURES I AM SO RENEWED
THAT ALL NATURE SEEMS RENEWED AROUND ME
AND WITH ME. THE SKY SEEMS TO BE A PURE,
A COOLER BLUE, THE TREES A DEEPER GREEN.
THE WHOLE WORLD IS CHARGED WITH THE
GLORY OF GOD, AND I FEEL FIRE AND
MUSIC UNDER MY FEET.

THOMAS MERTON

Love sought is good,
but given unsought is better.

WILLIAM SHAKESPEARE

*E*VERY GOOD GIFT AND EVERY
PERFECT GIFT IS FROM ABOVE.

JAMES 1:17

No one is poor who
had a godly mother.

ABRAHAM LINCOLN

$\mathcal{T}$HE BIBLE IS ONE OF THE GREATEST BLESSINGS
BESTOWED BY GOD ON THE CHILDREN OF MEN. . . .
IT IS ALL PURE, ALL SINCERE;
NOTHING TOO MUCH; NOTHING WANTING.

JOHN LOCKE

*To love and to be loved is
to feel the sun from both sides.*

DAVID VISCOTT

THE HERE, THE NOW, AND THE INDIVIDUAL HAVE
ALWAYS BEEN THE SPECIAL CONCERN OF THE
SAINT, THE ARTIST, THE POET—AND FROM TIME
IMMEMORIAL—THE WOMAN. IN THE SMALL CIRCLE
OF HOME SHE HAS NEVER QUITE FORGOTTEN
THE PARTICULAR UNIQUENESS OF EACH MEMBER
OF THE FAMILY; THE SPONTANEITY OF NOW;
THE VIVIDNESS OF HERE.
THIS IS THE BASIC SUBSTANCE OF LIFE.

ANNE MORROW LINDBERGH

Contentment is a perfect condition of life in which no aid or support is needed.

JOSEPH HENRY THAYER

A CHILD'S HAND IN YOURS—WHAT TENDERNESS
IT AROUSES, WHAT POWER IT CONJURES.
YOU ARE INSTANTLY THE VERY TOUCHSTONE
OF WISDOM AND STRENGTH.

MARJORIE HOLMES

It is as grandmothers that our mothers come into the fullness of their grace.

CHRISTOPHER MORLEY

*N*OTHING CONTRIBUTES MORE TO
CHEERFULNESS THAN THE HABIT OF
LOOKING AT THE GOOD SIDE OF THINGS.

WILLIAM B. ULLATHORNE

Casting all your care upon him;
for he careth for you.

1 Peter 5:7

FAITH IS THE VIRTUE BY WHICH,
CLINGING TO THE FAITHFULNESS OF GOD,
WE LEAN UPON HIM SO THAT WE MAY
OBTAIN WHAT HE GIVES US.

WILLIAM AMES

*N*OBODY CAN DO FOR LITTLE CHILDREN
WHAT GRANDPARENTS DO.
GRANDPARENTS SORT OF SPRINKLE STARDUST
OVER THE LIVES OF LITTLE CHILDREN.

ALEX HALEY

I DO THE VERY BEST I KNOW HOW—
THE VERY BEST I CAN; AND I MEAN TO KEEP
ON DOING SO UNTIL THE END.

ABRAHAM LINCOLN

OPTIMISM IS THE CHEERFUL FRAME OF MIND
THAT ENABLES A TEAKETTLE TO SING,
THOUGH IN HOT WATER UP TO ITS NOSE.

ANONYMOUS

*The most wasted of all days
is one without laughter.*

E. E. CUMMINGS

$\mathcal{J}$OY IS VERY INFECTIOUS;
THEREFORE, BE ALWAYS FULL OF JOY.

MOTHER TERESA

*W*e never become truly spiritual by sitting down and wishing to become so. You must undertake something so great that you cannot accomplish it unaided.

Phillips Brooks

A child reminds us that playtime is an essential part of our daily routine.

*T*HE SUBLIMEST SONG TO BE HEARD ON EARTH
IS THE LISPING OF THE HUMAN SOUL
ON THE LIPS OF CHILDREN.

VICTOR HUGO

DON'T YOU SEE THAT CHILDREN
ARE GOD'S BEST GIFT?

PSALM 127:3 MSG

*A*S FLOWERS CARRY DEWDROPS, TREMBLING ON
THE EDGES OF THE PETALS, AND READY TO FALL
AT THE FIRST WAFT OF THE WIND OR BRUSH OF BIRD,
SO THE HEART SHOULD CARRY ITS BEADED WORDS
OF THANKSGIVING. AT THE FIRST BREATH OF
HEAVENLY FLAVOR, LET DOWN THE SHOWER,
PERFUMED WITH THE HEART'S GRATITUDE.

HENRY WARD BEECHER

It's such a grand thing to be a mother of a mother—that's why the world calls her grandmother.

Unknown

I've learned that to be with those I like is enough.

WALT WHITMAN

*I*T IS BETTER TO HAVE NOBILITY OF CHARACTER
THAN NOBILITY OF BIRTH.

JEWISH PROVERB

THE CONSCIOUSNESS OF LOVING AND
BEING LOVED BRINGS A WARMTH AND RICHNESS
TO LIFE THAT NOTHING ELSE CAN BRING.

OSCAR WILDE

Big doesn't necessarily mean better.
Sunflowers aren't better than violets.

EDNA FERBER

Respect is love in plain clothes.

FRANKIE BYRNE

THE HEART SEES BETTER THAN THE EYE.

JEWISH PROVERB

Seize the day, and put the least possible trust in tomorrow.

HORACE

*E*NJOY THE LITTLE THINGS, FOR ONE DAY
YOU MAY LOOK BACK AND REALIZE
THEY WERE THE BIG THINGS.

ROBERT BRAULT

*T*RUST IN THE LORD WITH ALL THINE HEART; AND
LEAN NOT UNTO THINE OWN UNDERSTANDING.
IN ALL THY WAYS ACKNOWLEDGE HIM,
AND HE SHALL DIRECT THY PATHS.

PROVERBS 3:5-6

The seed of joy grows best
in a field of peace.

ROBERT J. WICKS

BE PATIENT WITH EVERYONE, BUT ABOVE
ALL WITH THYSELF. I MEAN, DO NOT BE
DISHEARTENED BY YOUR IMPERFECTIONS,
BUT ALWAYS RISE UP WITH FRESH COURAGE.

FRANCIS DE SALES

*H*AVE CONFIDENCE IN GOD'S MERCY,
FOR WHEN YOU THINK HE IS A LONG WAY
FROM YOU, HE IS OFTEN QUITE NEAR.

THOMAS À KEMPIS

*It is difficulties that
show what people are.*

Epicurus

*O*UR GREATEST GLORY CONSISTS NOT
IN NEVER FALLING, BUT IN RISING
EVERY TIME WE FALL.

OLIVER GOLDSMITH

*E*VERYTHING WE CALL A TRIAL,
A SORROW, OR A DUTY, BELIEVE ME
THAT AN ANGEL'S HAND IS THERE.

FRA GIOVANNI

Faith consists in believing when it is beyond the power of reason to believe.

VOLTAIRE

Never be afraid to trust an unknown future to a known God.

CORRIE TEN BOOM

COMMIT TO THE LORD WHATEVER YOU DO,
AND YOUR PLANS WILL SUCCEED.

PROVERBS 16:3 NIV

*H*OPE IS LIKE THE SUN,
WHICH, AS WE JOURNEY TOWARD IT,
CASTS THE SHADOW OF OUR BURDEN BEHIND US.

SAMUEL SMILES

IF YOU WANT YOUR NEIGHBOR TO SEE
WHAT THE CHRIST SPIRIT WILL DO FOR HIM,
LET HIM SEE WHAT IT HAS DONE FOR YOU.

HENRY WARD BEECHER

No act of kindness,
no matter how small, is ever wasted.

AESOP

GRANDMOTHERS ARE JUST
ANTIQUE LITTLE GIRLS.

UNKNOWN

*H*E WHO CANNOT FORGIVE OTHERS
DESTROYS THE BRIDGE OVER WHICH
HE HIMSELF MUST PASS.

GEORGE HERBERT

Nothing great was ever achieved without enthusiasm.

RALPH WALDO EMERSON

*Y*OUR ATTITUDE ABOUT WHO YOU ARE AND
WHAT YOU HAVE IS A VERY LITTLE THING
THAT MAKES A VERY BIG DIFFERENCE.

THEODORE ROOSEVELT

Cherish all your happy moments;
they make a fine cushion for old age.

BOOTH TARKINGTON

I joy to see myself now live:
this age best pleaseth me!

ROBERT HERRICK

*F*EAR LESS, HOPE MORE; EAT LESS,
CHEW MORE; WHINE LESS, BREATHE MORE;
TALK LESS, SAY MORE; LOVE MORE,
AND ALL GOOD THINGS WILL BE YOURS.

SWEDISH PROVERB

$\mathcal{L}$ET ME TELL THEE, TIME IS A VERY PRECIOUS
GIFT FROM GOD; SO PRECIOUS THAT IT'S
ONLY GIVEN TO US MOMENT BY MOMENT.

AMELIA BARR

One enemy is too many;
a hundred friends too few.

ANONYMOUS

121

*W*HEN A GREAT ADVENTURE IS OFFERED,
YOU DON'T REFUSE IT.

AMELIA EARHART

A cheerful heart is good medicine.

PROVERBS 17:22 NIV

Perfect love sometimes does not come until the first grandchild.

WELSH PROVERB

IT IS ASTONISHING HOW SHORT A TIME
IT TAKES FOR VERY WONDERFUL
THINGS TO HAPPEN.

FRANCES HODGSON BURNETT

*P*OPSICLES. COOKIES. LOLLIPOPS.
SOME OF LIFE'S MOST EFFECTIVE REMEDIES.

BONNIE JENSEN

We must laugh and we must sing,
we are blest by everything.

WILLIAM BUTLER YEATS

*C*ARVE YOUR NAME ON HEARTS
AND NOT ON MARBLE.

CHARLES H. SPURGEON

Love is a great beautifier.

LOUISA MAY ALCOTT

Generally, by the time you are Real,
most of your hair has been loved off,
and your eyes drop out and you
get loose in the joints and very shabby.
But these things don't matter at all,
because once you are real you can't be ugly,
except to people who don't understand.

Margery Williams, *The Velveteen Rabbit*

IF BECOMING A GRANDMOTHER WAS ONLY
A MATTER OF CHOICE, I SHOULD ADVISE EVERY
ONE OF YOU STRAIGHTAWAY TO BECOME ONE.
THERE IS NO FUN FOR OLD PEOPLE LIKE IT!

HANNAH WHITALL SMITH

Love never fails.

1 CORINTHIANS 13:8 NIV

We ARE SHAPED AND
FASHIONED BY WHAT WE LOVE.

JOHANN WOLFGANG VON GOETHE

God gave us memories that we might have roses in December.

JAMES M. BARRIE

ONE CAN NEVER SPEAK ENOUGH
OF THE VIRTUES. . .
THE POWER OF SHARED LAUGHTER.

FRANÇOISE SAGAN

*A*NGELS FLY BECAUSE THEY
TAKE THEMSELVES LIGHTLY.

UNKNOWN

Life is what we make it.
Always has been, always will be.

GRANDMA MOSES

INTO ALL OUR LIVES, IN MANY SIMPLE,
FAMILIAR, HOMELY WAYS, GOD INFUSES THIS
ELEMENT OF JOY FROM THE SURPRISES OF LIFE,
WHICH UNEXPECTEDLY BRIGHTEN OUR DAYS,
AND FILL OUR EYES WITH LIGHT.

HENRY WADSWORTH LONGFELLOW

*W*HEN GRACE IS JOINED WITH WRINKLES,
IT IS ADORABLE. THERE IS AN UNSPEAKABLE
DAWN IN HAPPY OLD AGE.

VICTOR HUGO

*God has given us
these times of joy.*

PSALM 81:4 TLB

GRANDMOTHER-GRANDCHILD RELATIONSHIPS
ARE SIMPLE. GRANDMAS ARE SHORT ON
CRITICISM AND LONG ON LOVE.

UNKNOWN

Those who bring sunshine
to the lives of others
cannot keep it from themselves.

JAMES M. BARRIE

TO BE GLAD OF LIFE BECAUSE IT GIVES YOU
THE CHANCE TO LOVE AND TO WORK AND
TO PLAY AND TO LOOK UP AT THE STARS. . . .
TO THINK. . .OFTEN OF YOUR FRIENDS,
AND EVERY DAY OF CHRIST. . .THESE ARE LITTLE
GUIDEPOSTS ON THE FOOTPATH OF PEACE.

HENRY VAN DYKE

Laugh, if you are wise.

LATIN PROVERB

*T*HE BEST PORTIONS OF A GOOD LIFE
ARE THE LITTLE, NAMELESS, UNREMEMBERED
ACTS OF KINDNESS AND LOVE WE DO FOR OTHERS.

WILLIAM WORDSWORTH

FORGIVE, FORGET. BEAR WITH THE FAULTS
OF OTHERS AS YOU WOULD HAVE THEM BEAR
WITH YOURS. BE PATIENT AND UNDERSTANDING.

PHILLIPS BROOKS

$\mathcal{R}$EMEMBER NOT ONLY TO SAY
THE RIGHT THING IN THE RIGHT PLACE,
BUT FAR MORE DIFFICULT STILL,
TO LEAVE UNSAID THE WRONG THING
AT THE TEMPTING MOMENT.

BENJAMIN FRANKLIN

$\mathcal{T}$HREE THINGS IN HUMAN LIFE ARE IMPORTANT:
THE FIRST IS TO BE KIND.
THE SECOND IS TO BE KIND.
AND THE THIRD IS TO BE KIND.

HENRY JAMES

GOD HAS GIVEN EACH OF YOU SOME
SPECIAL ABILITIES; BE SURE TO USE THEM TO
HELP EACH OTHER, PASSING ON TO OTHERS
GOD'S MANY KINDS OF BLESSINGS.

1 PETER 4:10 TLB

*A garden of love grows
in a grandmother's heart.*

UNKNOWN

*W*ORRY DOES NOT EMPTY
TOMORROW OF ITS SORROW.
IT EMPTIES TODAY OF ITS STRENGTH.

CORRIE TEN BOOM

GUARD WELL YOUR SPARE MOMENTS.
THEY ARE LIKE UNCUT DIAMONDS.
DISCARD THEM AND THEIR VALUE WILL NEVER
BE KNOWN. IMPROVE THEM AND THEY WILL
BECOME THE BRIGHTEST GEMS IN A USEFUL LIFE.

RALPH WALDO EMERSON

$\mathcal{F}$EELING GRATITUDE AND NOT EXPRESSING IT
IS LIKE WRAPPING A PRESENT
AND NOT GIVING IT.

WILLIAM ARTHUR WARD

IT IS FOR US TO PRAY NOT FOR TASKS
EQUAL TO OUR POWERS, BUT FOR POWERS
EQUAL TO OUR TASKS, TO GO FORWARD
WITH A GREAT DESIRE FOREVER BEATING
AT THE DOOR OF OUR HEARTS AS WE
TRAVEL TOWARD OUR DISTANT GOAL.

HELEN KELLER

When the solution is simple,
God is answering.

ALBERT EINSTEIN

*E*VERY NOW AND THEN GO AWAY, HAVE A LITTLE RELAXATION; FOR WHEN YOU COME BACK TO YOUR WORK, YOUR JUDGMENT WILL BE SURER.

LEONARDO DA VINCI

GRANDMOTHERS AND ROSES
ARE MUCH THE SAME.
EACH ARE GOD'S MASTERPIECES
WITH DIFFERENT NAMES.

UNKNOWN

$\mathcal{T}$RUST SHOULD BE IN THE LIVING GOD
WHO ALWAYS RICHLY GIVES US
ALL WE NEED FOR OUR ENJOYMENT.

1 TIMOTHY 6:17 TLB

*R*EAD, EVERY DAY, SOMETHING NO ONE ELSE
IS READING. THINK, EVERY DAY, SOMETHING
NO ONE ELSE IS THINKING. DO, EVERY DAY,
SOMETHING NO ONE ELSE WOULD BE SILLY
ENOUGH TO DO. IT IS BAD FOR THE MIND
TO BE ALWAYS PART OF UNANIMITY.

CHRISTOPHER MORLEY

Light tomorrow with today!

ELIZABETH BARRETT BROWNING

$\mathcal{P}$RAY, AND LET GOD WORRY.

MARTIN LUTHER

*A good laugh is
sunshine in a house.*

WILLIAM MAKEPEACE THACKERAY

A KEEN SENSE OF HUMOR HELPS US TO
OVERLOOK THE UNBECOMING, UNDERSTAND
THE UNCONVENTIONAL, TOLERATE THE
UNPLEASANT, OVERCOME THE UNEXPECTED,
AND OUTLAST THE UNBEARABLE.

BILLY GRAHAM

*Whatsoever things are lovely. . .
think on these things.*

$\mathcal{L}$ET NOTHING DISTURB YOU, LET NOTHING FRIGHTEN YOU: EVERYTHING PASSES AWAY EXCEPT GOD; GOD ALONE IS SUFFICIENT.

TERESA OF AVILA

A grandmother is a little bit parent,
a little bit teacher,
and a little bit best friend.

UNKNOWN

$\mathcal{T}$HE BEST THINGS ARE NEAREST:
BREATH IN YOUR NOSTRILS, LIGHT IN YOUR EYES,
FLOWERS AT YOUR FEET, DUTIES AT YOUR HAND,
THE PATH OF GOD JUST BEFORE YOU.

ROBERT LOUIS STEVENSON

*There is nothing that makes us love
a man so much as praying for him.*

WILLIAM LAW

*G*OD WRITES THE GOSPEL NOT IN THE
BIBLE ALONE, BUT ON TREES AND
FLOWERS AND CLOUDS AND STARS.

MARTIN LUTHER

*P*LEASURE IS VERY SELDOM FOUND WHERE
IT IS SOUGHT. OUR BRIGHTEST BLAZES ARE
COMMONLY KINDLED BY UNEXPECTED SPARKS.

SAMUEL JOHNSON

*W*E DO NOT NEED TO SEARCH FOR HEAVEN,
OVER HERE OR OVER THERE, IN ORDER TO FIND
OUR ETERNAL FATHER. IN FACT, WE DO NOT EVEN
NEED TO SPEAK OUT LOUD, FOR THOUGH WE SPEAK
IN THE SMALLEST WHISPER OR THE MOST FLEETING
THOUGHT, HE IS CLOSE ENOUGH TO HEAR US.

TERESA OF AVILA

The world is charged with
the grandeur of God.

GERARD MANLEY HOPKINS

*T*HE CREATION OF A THOUSAND
FORESTS IS IN ONE ACORN.

RALPH WALDO EMERSON

LIVE YOUR LIFE WHILE YOU HAVE IT.
LIFE IS A SPLENDID GIFT–
THERE IS NOTHING SMALL ABOUT IT.

FLORENCE NIGHTINGALE

In prayer it is better to have a heart without words than words without a heart.

JOHN BUNYAN

Let your conversation be
always full of grace.

COLOSSIANS 4:6 NIV

A GENTLE WORD, A KIND LOOK,
A GOOD-NATURED SMILE CAN WORK
WONDERS AND ACCOMPLISH MIRACLES.

WILLIAM HAZLITT

*Let us not hurry so in our pace of living
that we lose sight of the art of living.*

FRANCIS BACON

*W*HERE THE SOUL IS FULL OF PEACE AND JOY,
OUTWARD SURROUNDINGS AND CIRCUMSTANCES
ARE OF COMPARATIVELY LITTLE ACCOUNT.

HANNAH WHITALL SMITH

The greatest use for life
is to spend it for something
that will outlast it.

WILLIAM JAMES

GRANDCHILDREN ARE GOD'S COMPENSATION
FOR GRAY HAIR AND WRINKLES.

UNKNOWN

A WORD SPOKEN IN DUE SEASON,
HOW GOOD IS IT!

PROVERBS 15:23

It takes a village to raise a child.

*W*HAT THE HEART HAS ONCE OWNED
AND HAD, IT SHALL NEVER LOSE.

HENRY WARD BEECHER